Respect the Rules!

Gail Skroback Hennessey, M.S.T.

Consultants

Shelley Scudder
Gifted Education Teacher
Broward County Schools

Caryn Williams, M.S.Ed.
Madison County Schools
Huntsville, AL

Publishing Credits

Dona Herweck Rice, *Editor-in-Chief*
Lee Aucoin, *Creative Director*
Torrey Maloof, *Editor*
Diana Kenney, M.A.Ed., NBCT,
    Associate Education Editor
Marissa Rodriguez, *Designer*
Stephanie Reid, *Photo Editor*
Rachelle Cracchiolo, M.S.Ed., *Publisher*

Teacher Created Materials

5301 Oceanus Drive
Huntington Beach, CA 92649-1030
http://www.tcmpub.com
ISBN 978-1-4333-6971-1
© 2014 Teacher Created Materials, Inc.

Table of Contents

What Is a Rule?

Rules tell us what we may and may not do. Rules should be **equal** (EE-kwuhl) for all people.

A boy reads the rules at a pool.

The Constitution

The Constitution (kon-sti-TOO-shuhn) is a list of rules for the United States of America.

United States Constitution

Rules Are Important

Rules **protect** us. They keep us safe.
They help us work together.

These rules help kids work together at school.

The crossing guard helps the kids cross the street safely.

Without rules, people might make bad choices. Cars might not stop at red lights. People might fight.

Drawing on a wall is a bad choice.

Fighting is a bad choice, too.

Who Makes Rules?

Principals make rules for schools.
Teachers make rules for classrooms.
Parents make rules for homes.

The teacher tells the rules to her class.

Rules for Our Country

Government (GUHV-ern-muhnt) leaders make rules for our country. These rules are called **laws**.

This is Capitol Hill in Washington, DC. It is where government leaders make the rules for our country.

Follow the Rules

Who makes sure we follow the rules?
Parents do. Teachers do. The police do.

This police officer makes sure people follow the rules.

These teachers make sure their students follow the rules in 1940.

When we do not follow a rule, there is a **consequence** (KON-si-kwens), or result. We learn to follow the rule next time.

This girl did not follow the rules.
She has to stay after class.

Good Job!

When you follow the rules in school, you may earn rewards.

Brooke has earned three stars!

It Is Golden

The **Golden Rule** is very old. It says to treat others the way you want to be treated.

This girl helps a friend who is hurt.

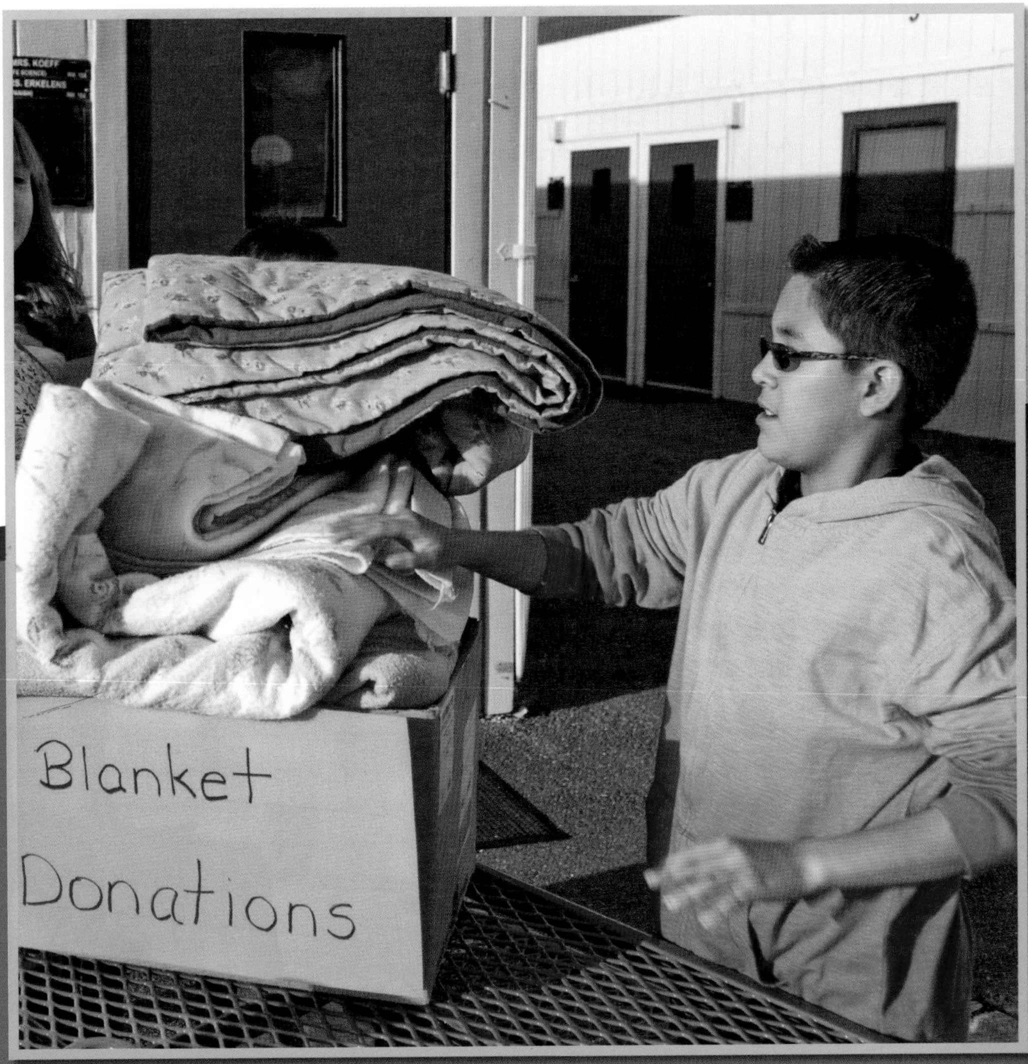

This boy collects blankets to give to people in need.

Show Respect

When you follow the rules, you show **respect** (ri-SPEKT). You show respect for yourself. You show respect for others.

Kids can show respect by waiting in line.

Students wait in line in 1936.

List It!

Think of the rules you have at home. Talk about the rules with your family. Make a list of the rules. Find a place to hang your list to help everyone remember the rules.

This family writes a list of rules.

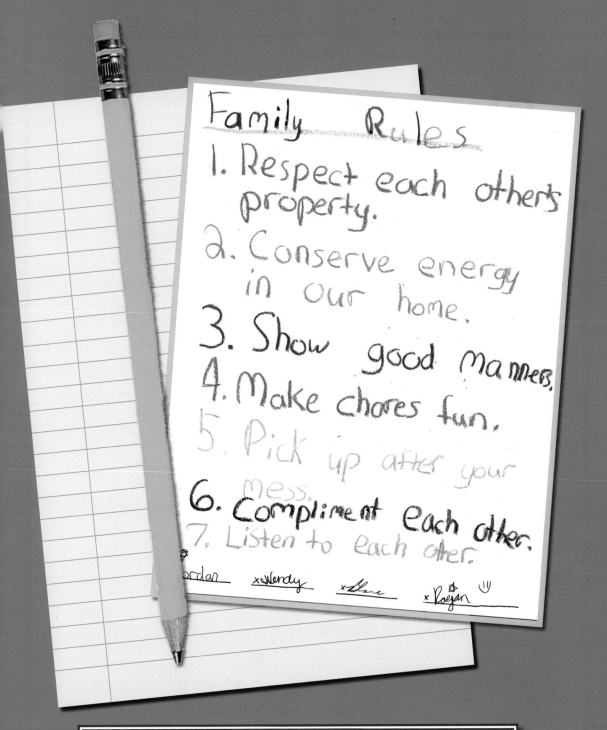

Family Rules

1. Respect each others property.
2. Conserve energy in our home.
3. Show good manners.
4. Make chores fun.
5. Pick up after your mess.
6. Compliment each other.
7. Listen to each other.

x Jordan   x Wendy   x Diane   x Roejan

This is a family's list of rules.

Glossary

consequence—a result

equal—the same

Golden Rule—a rule that says to treat others the way you want to be treated

government—a group of people who make choices for a country

laws—a set of rules made by a government

protect—to keep safe

respect—the way you show that someone or something is important

rules—things that tell what you may or may not do

Index

Your Turn!

My Class Rules!

This teacher is telling her class about rules. What rules do you have in your class? Talk to a friend about your class rules. Write them down.